CLASSICAL THEMES
FOR BANJO

ARRANGED BY MARK PHILLIPS AND JIM SCHUSTEDT

CONTENTS

ISBN 978-1-4950-1464-2

HAL•LEONARD®
CORPORATION
7777 W. BLUEMOUND RD. P.O. BOX 13819 MILWAUKEE, WI 53213

In Australia Contact:
Hal Leonard Australia Pty. Ltd.
4 Lentara Court
Cheltenham, Victoria, 3192 Australia
Email: ausadmin@halleonard.com.au

Visit Hal Leonard Online at
www.halleonard.com

Ave Maria

By Franz Schubert

G tuning:
(5th-1st) G-D-G-B-D

Key of G

Moderately slow, in 2

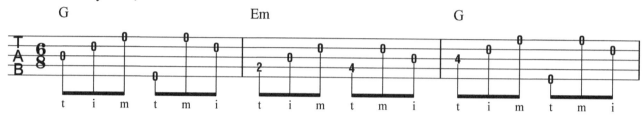

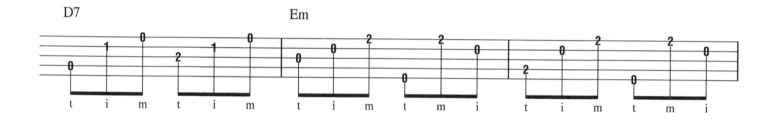

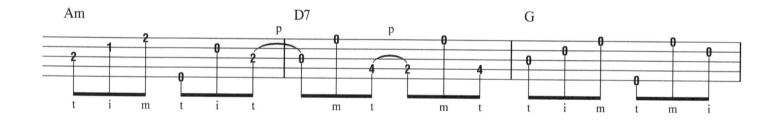

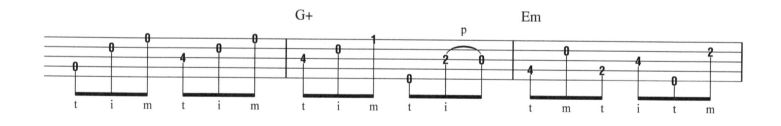

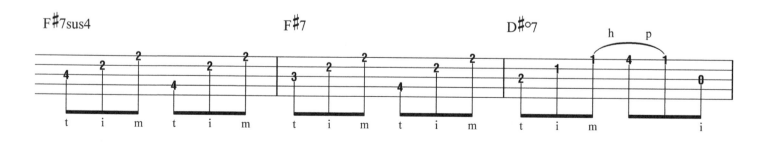

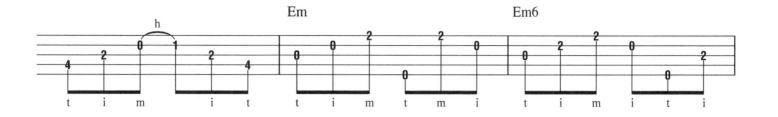

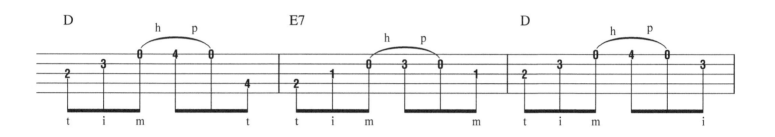

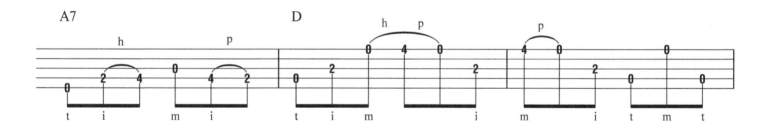

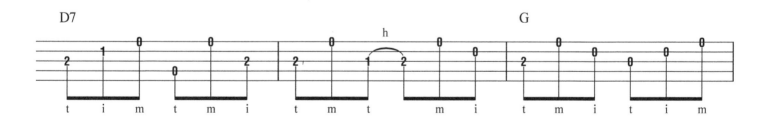

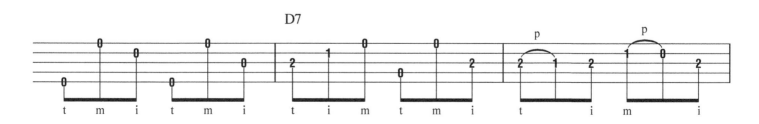

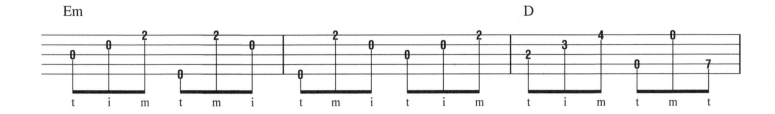

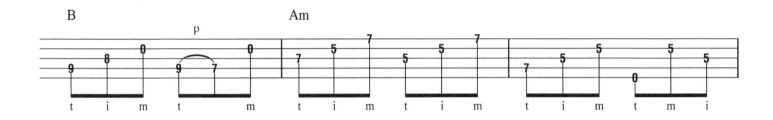

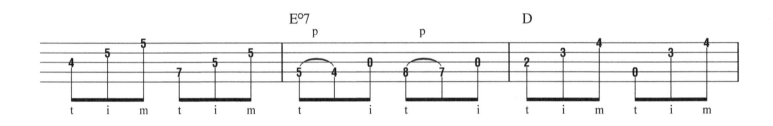

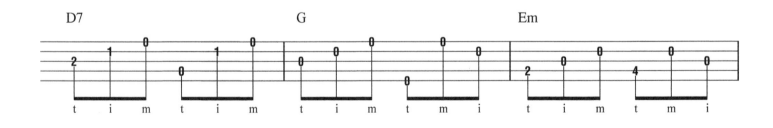

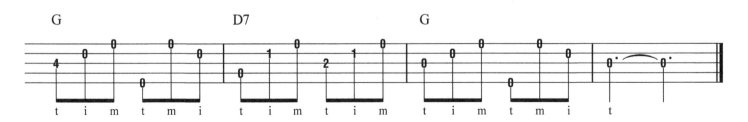

Ave Maria
(Based on "Prelude in C" by Johann Sebastian Bach)
By Charles Gounod

G Tuning:
(5th-1st) G-D-G-B-D

Key of G

Moderately slow

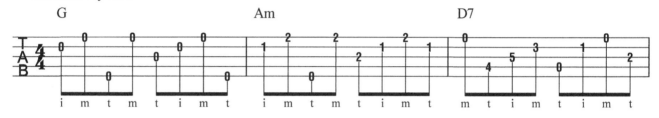

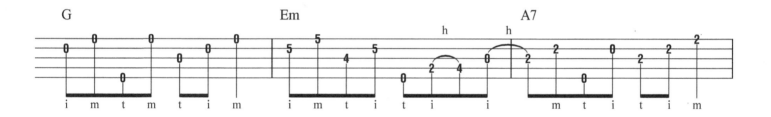

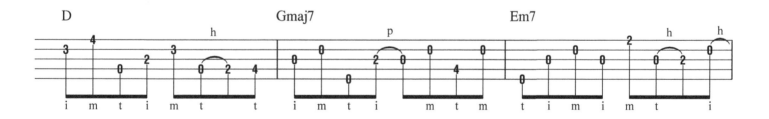

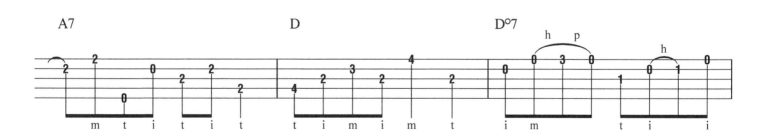

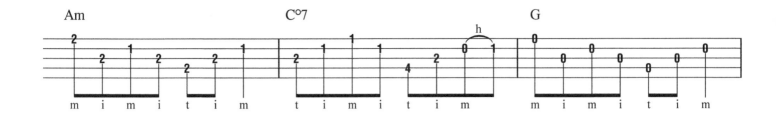

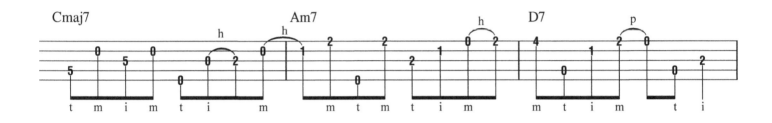

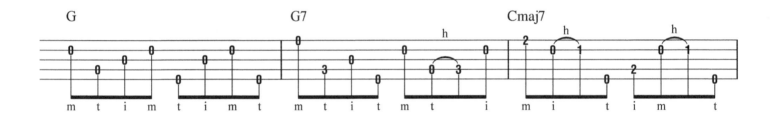

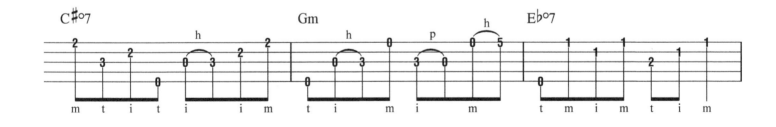

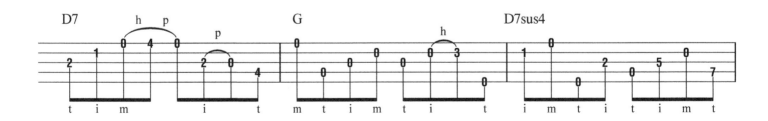

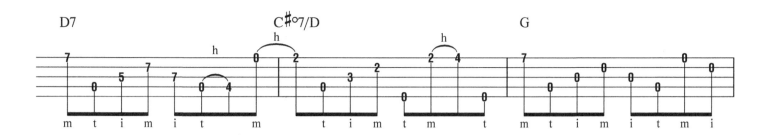

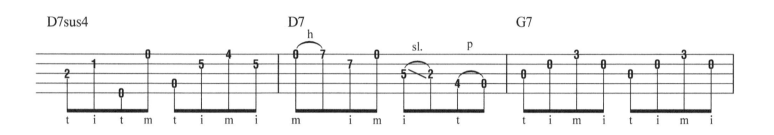

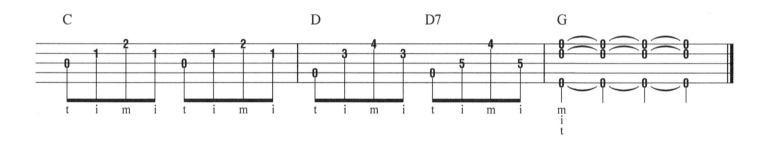

Air on the G String

By Johann Sebastian Bach

G tuning:
(5th–1st) G-D-G-B-D

Key of C

Slowly

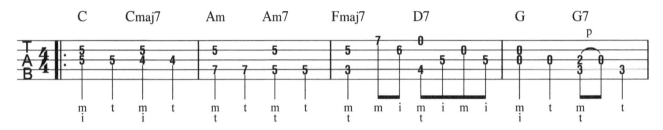

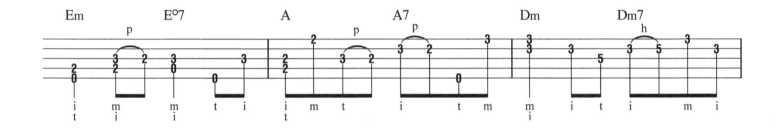

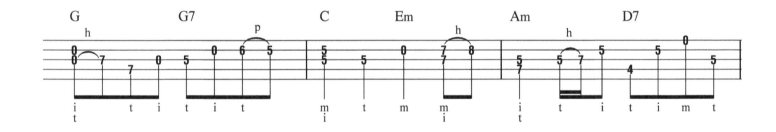

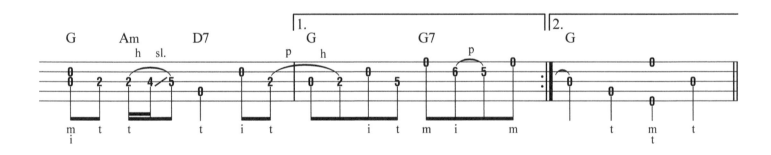

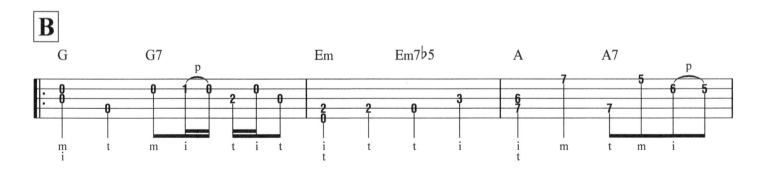

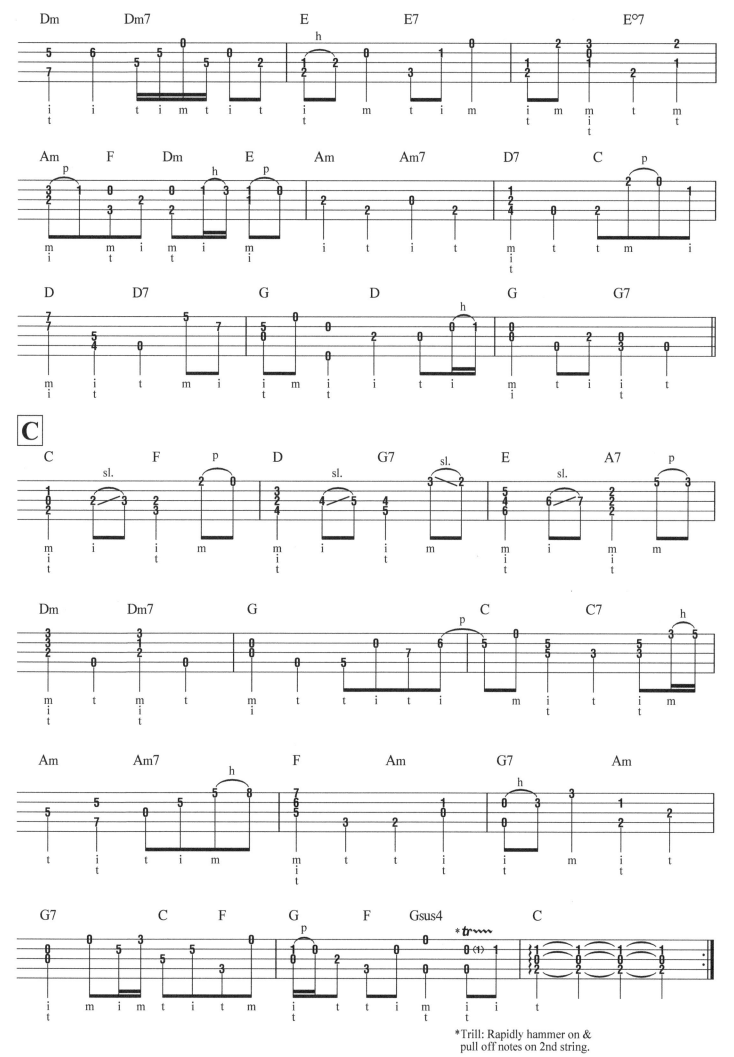

*Trill: Rapidly hammer on &
pull off notes on 2nd string.

Dance of the Hours
(from *La Gioconda*)

By A. Ponchielli

G tuning:
(5th-1st) G-D-G-B-D

Key of G

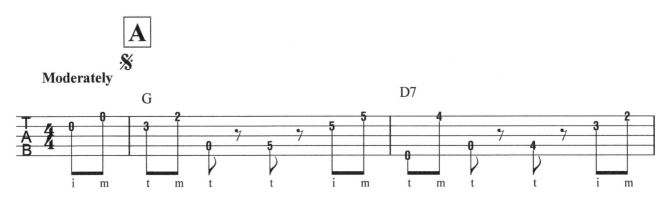

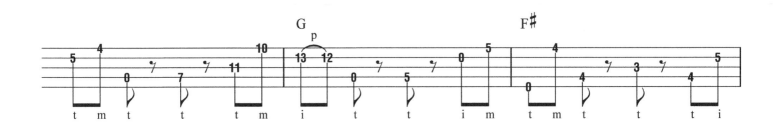

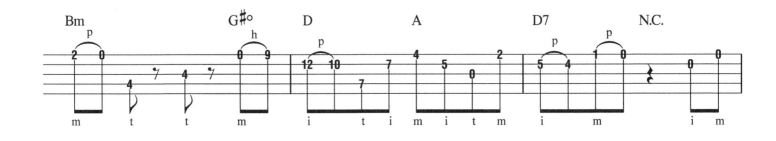

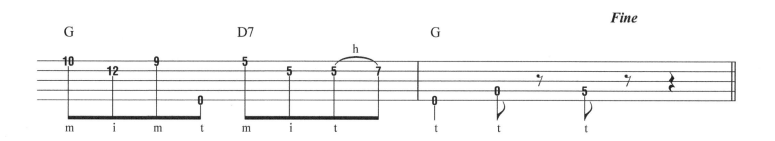

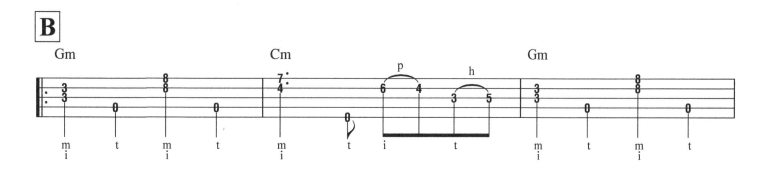

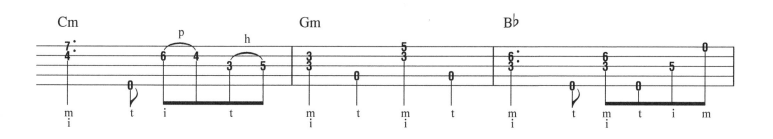

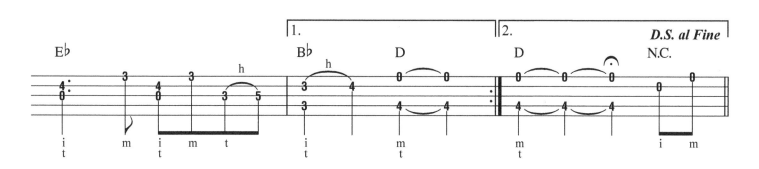

Für Elise

By Ludwig van Beethoven

G tuning:
(5th-1st) G-D-G-B-D

Key of E minor

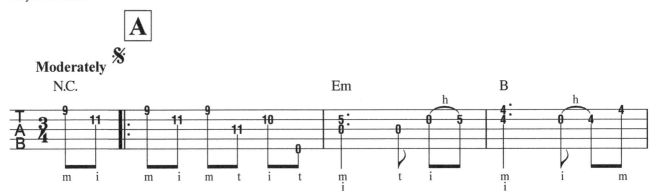

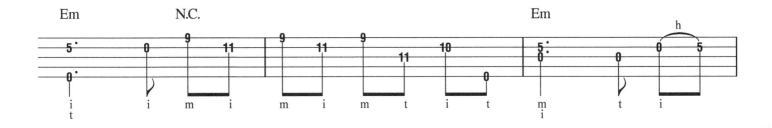

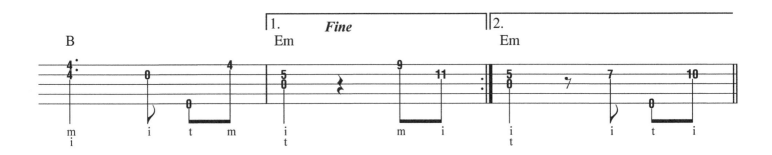

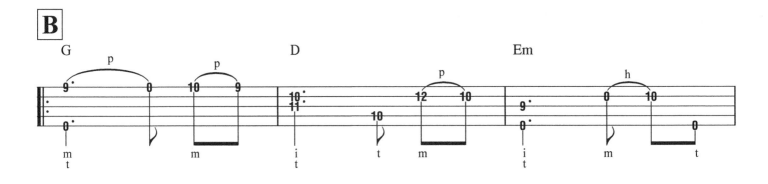

The Happy Farmer

By Robert Schumann

Tuning:
(5th-1st) G-D-G-B-D

Key of G

Brightly

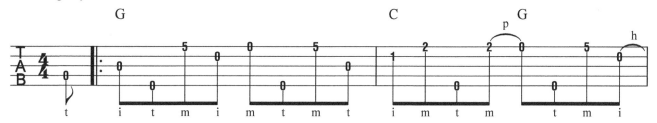

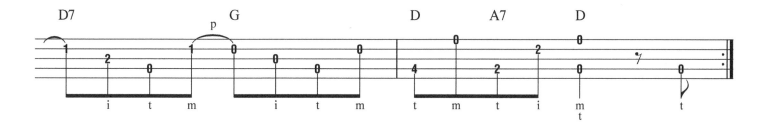

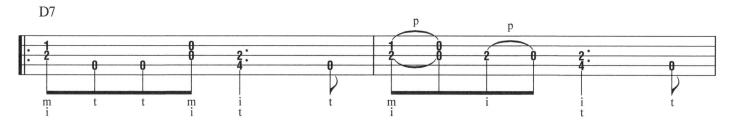

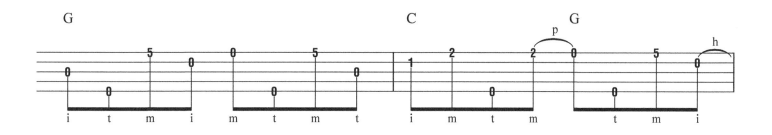

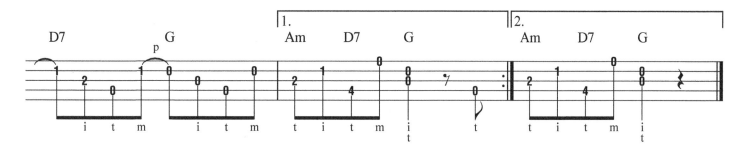

Harmonious Blacksmith

By George Frideric Handel

G tuning:
(5th-1st) G-D-G-B-D

Key of G

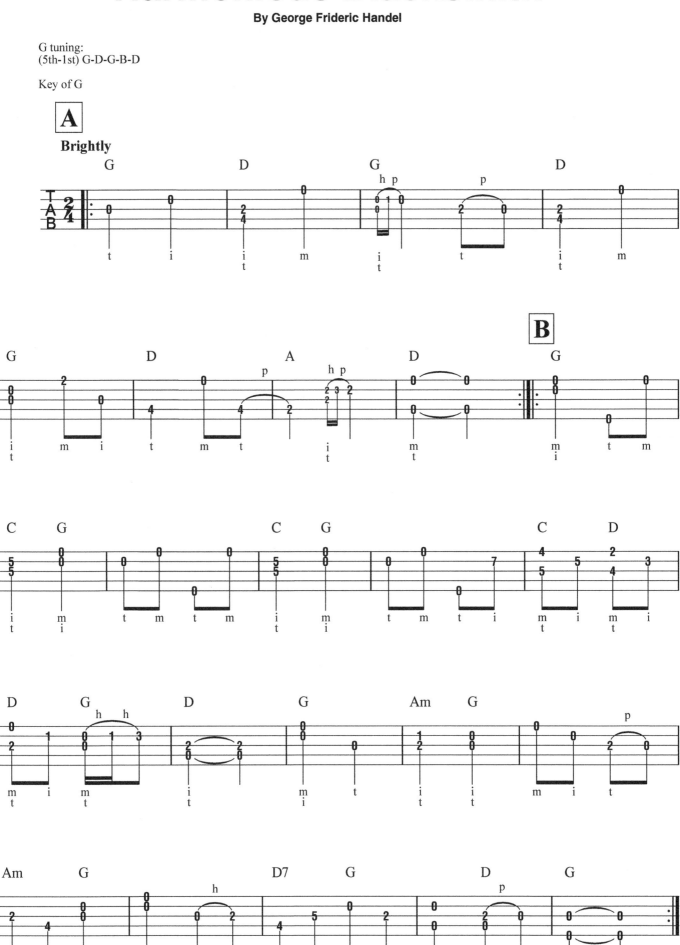

In the Hall of the Mountain King
(from *Peer Gynt*)
By Edvard Grieg

G tuning:
(5th-1st) G-D-G-B-D

Key of E minor

March tempo

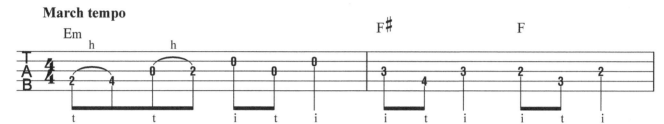

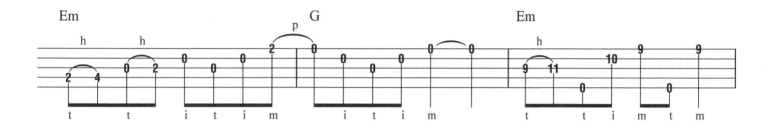

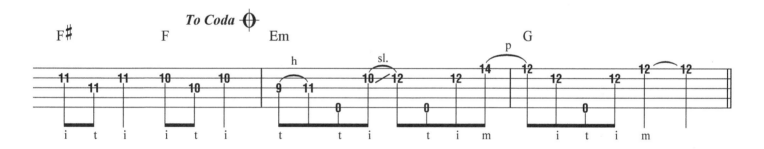

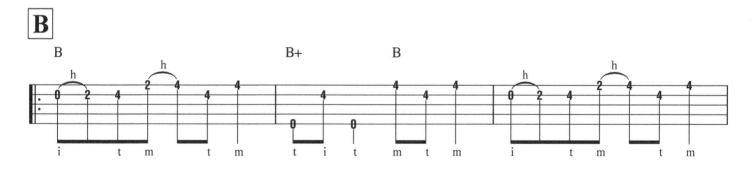

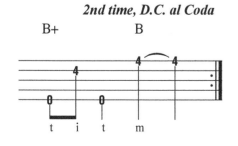

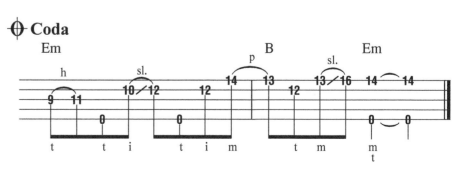

Jesu, Joy of Man's Desiring

(from Cantata No. 147)

By Johann Sebastian Bach

G tuning:
(5th-1st) G-D-G-B-D

Key of G

Moderately slow

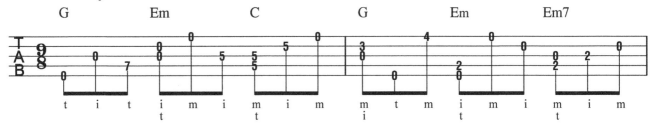

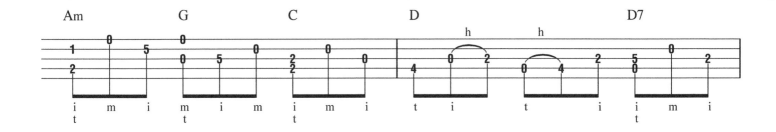

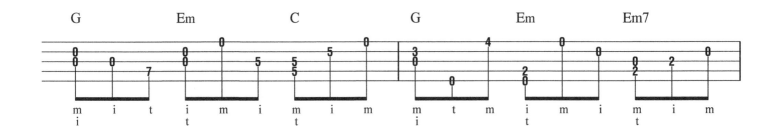

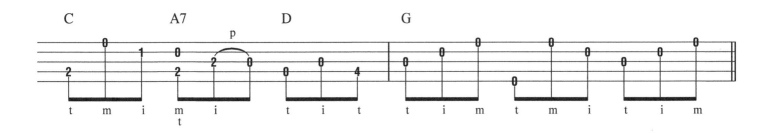

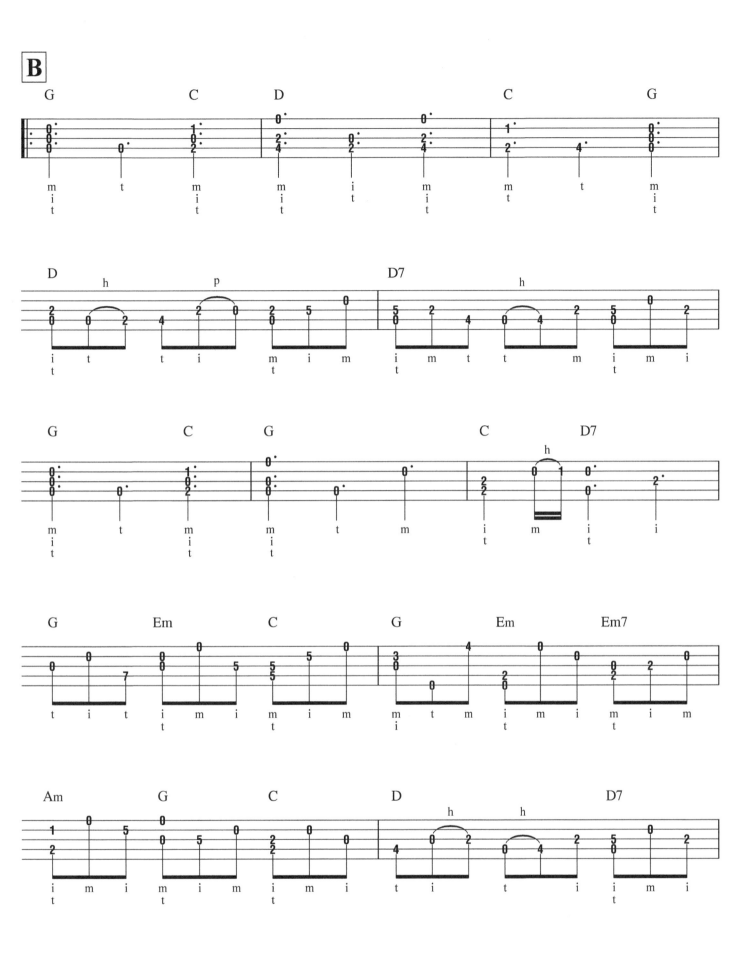
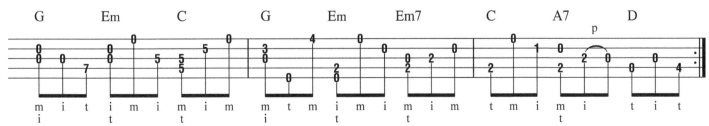

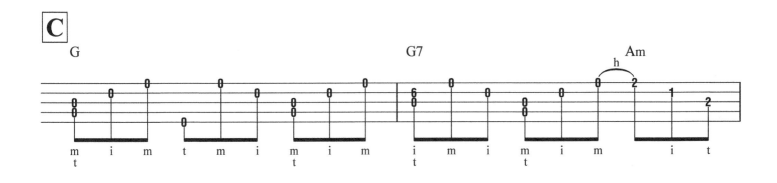

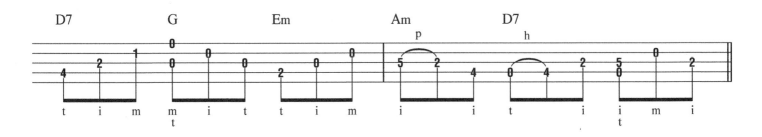

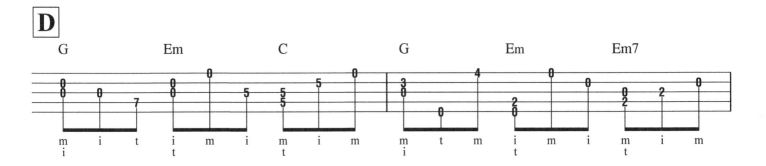

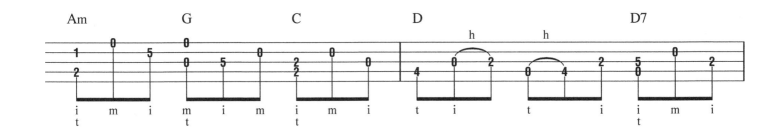

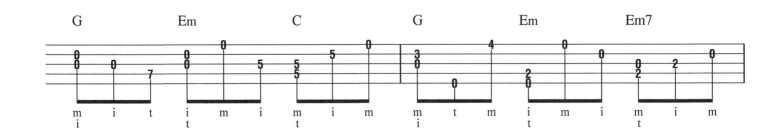

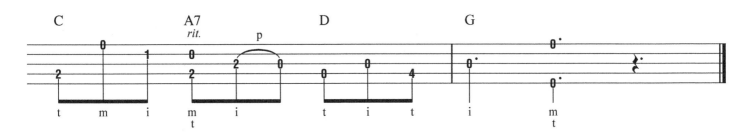

Spring
(from *The Four Seasons*)

By Antonio Vivaldi

G tuning:
(5th-1st) G-D-G-B-D

Key of C

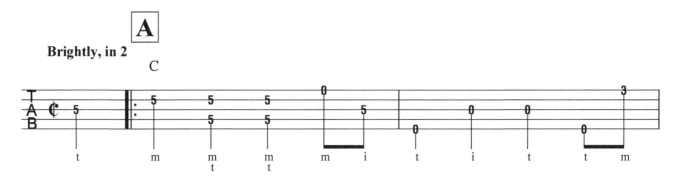

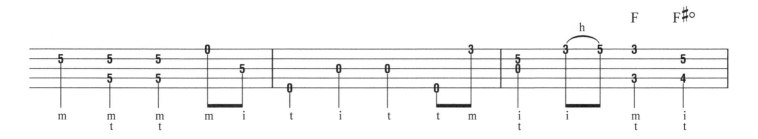

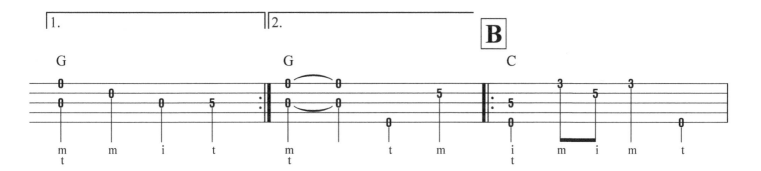

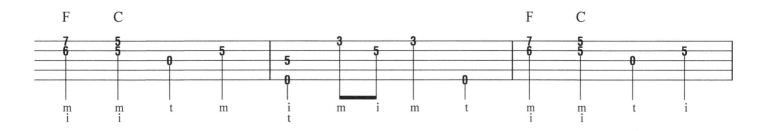

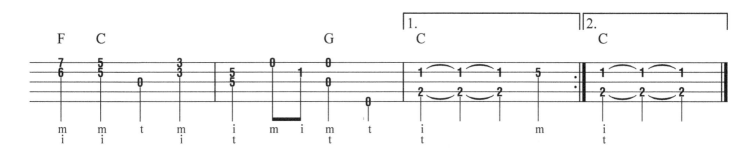

Minuet
(from String Quintet in E Major)
By Luigi Boccherini

G tuning:
(5th-1st) G-D-G-B-D

Key of C

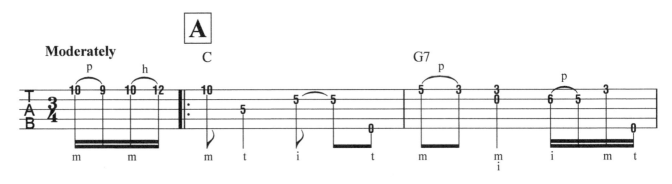

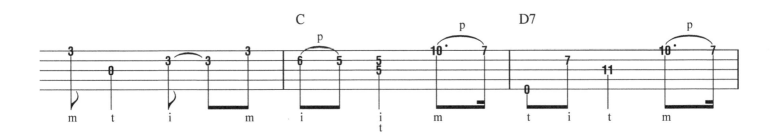

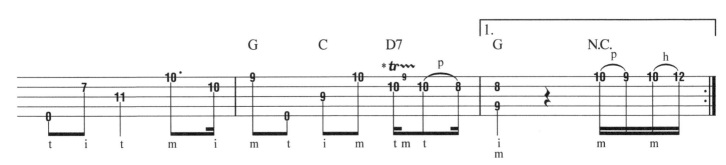

*Trill: Pick 2nd & 1st strings
alternately in rapid succession.

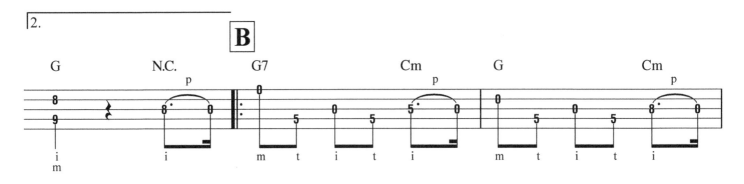

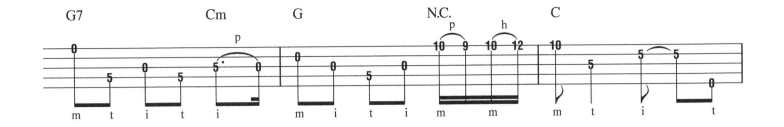

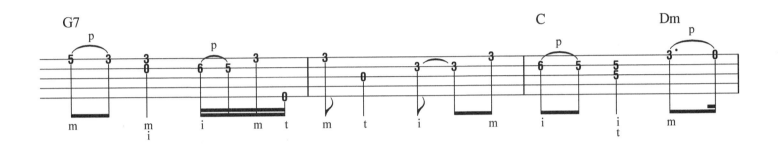

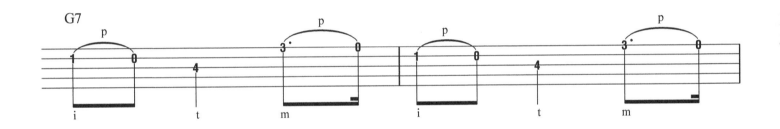

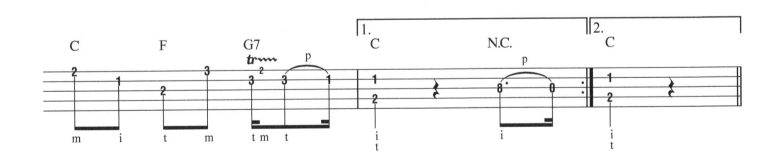

Ode to Joy
(from Symphony No. 9, Fourth Movement Choral Theme)

By Ludwig van Beethoven

G tuning:
(5th-1st) G-D-G-B-D

Key of C

Moderately fast

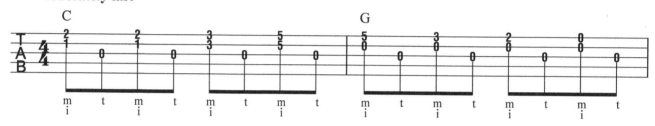

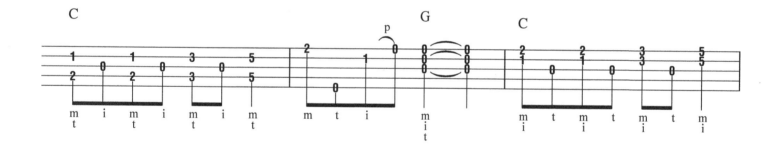

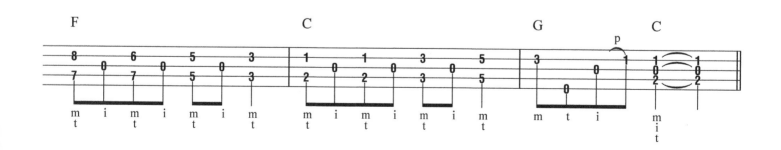

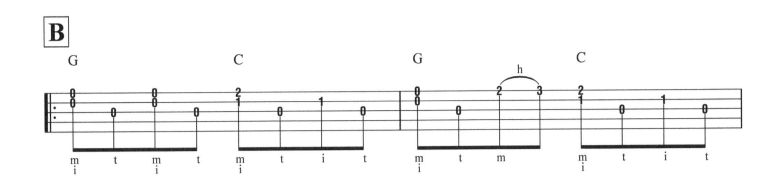

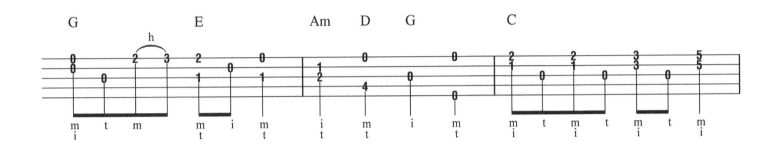

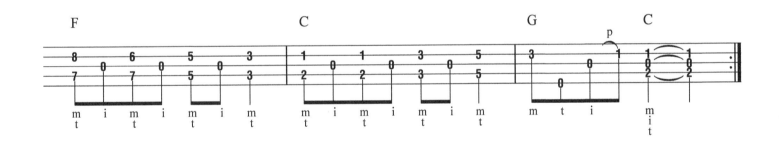

Pachelbel's Canon
(Canon in D)
By Johann Pachelbel

Tuning:
(5th-1st) G-D-G-B-D

Key of G

Slowly

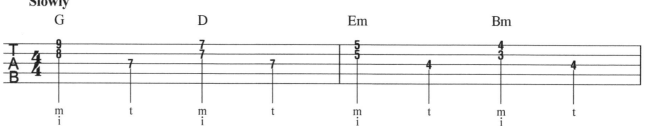

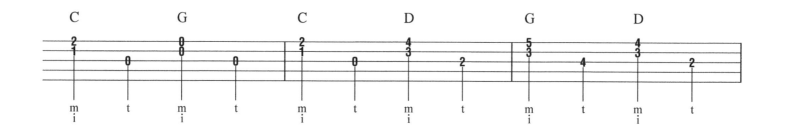

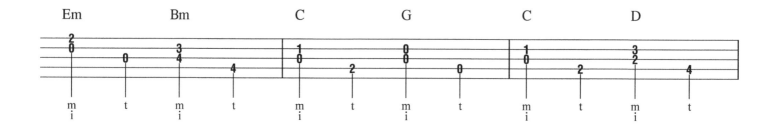

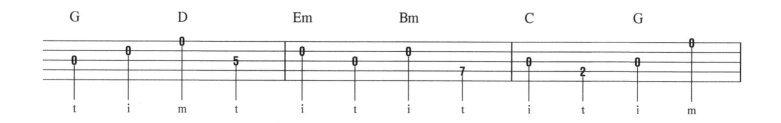

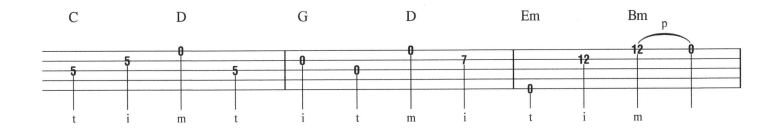

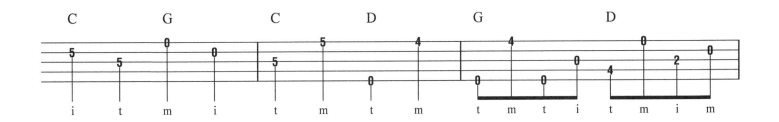

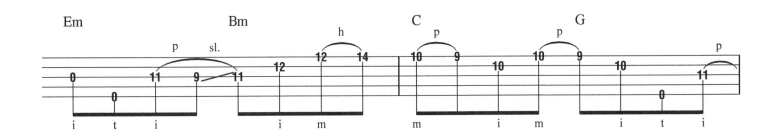

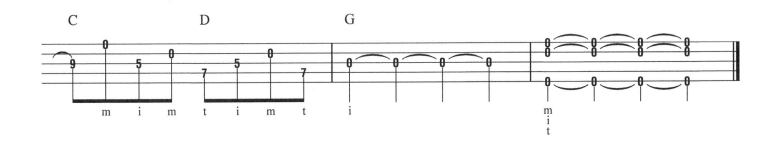

Pomp and Circumstance

By Edward Elgar

G tuning:
(5th-1st) G-D-G-B-D

Key of G

Moderately, marchlike

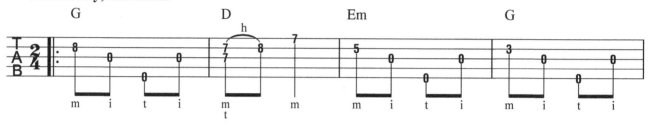

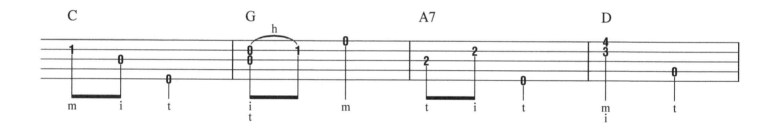

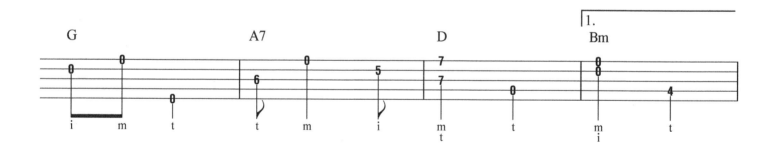

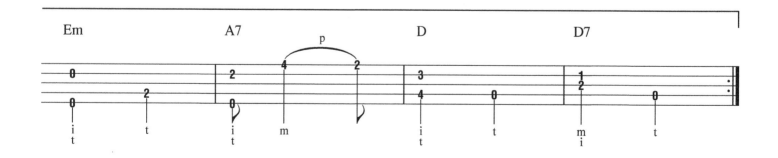

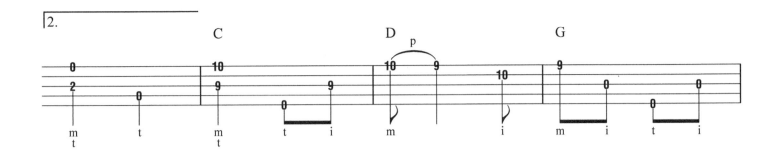

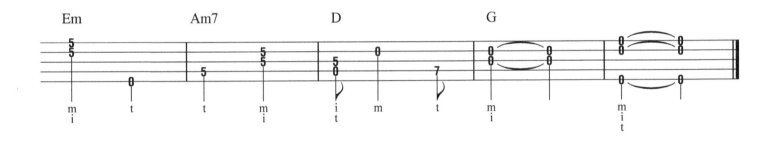

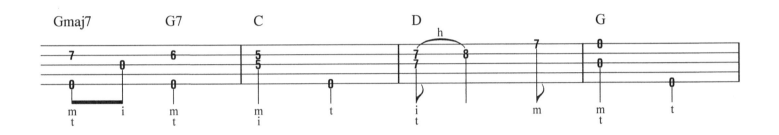

Rondeau

By Jean-Joseph Mouret

G tuning:
(5th-1st) G-D-G-B-D

Key of C

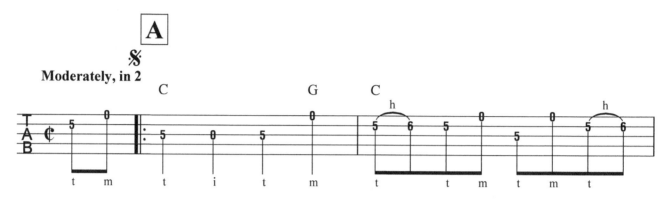

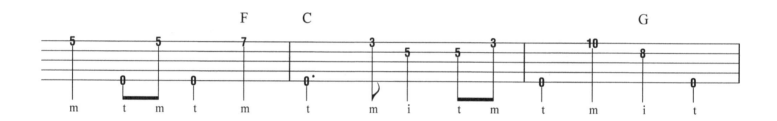

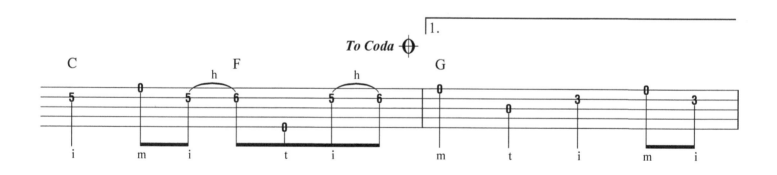

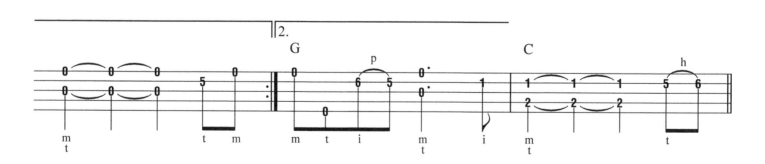

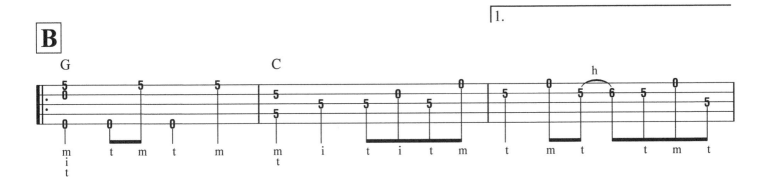

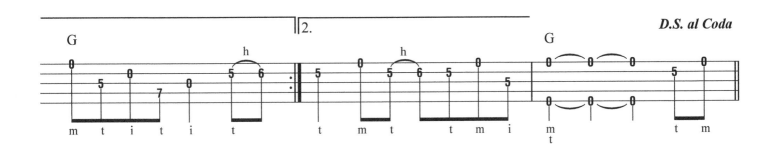

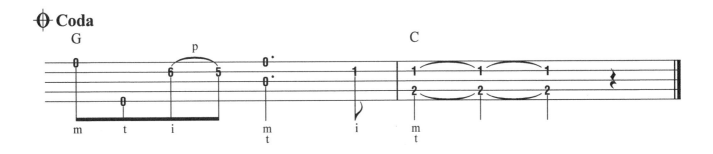

Symphony No. 40 in G Minor
(First Movement Excerpt)

By Wolfgang Amadeus Mozart

G minor tuning:
(5th-1st) G-D-G-B♭-D

Key of G minor

Moderately fast

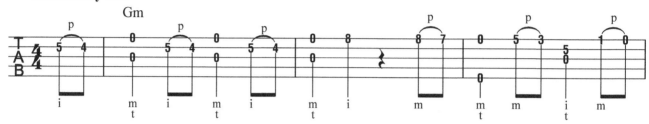

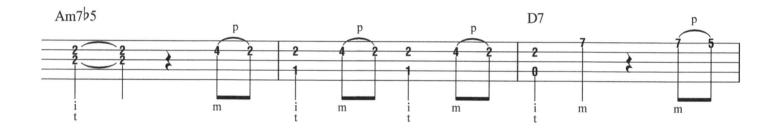

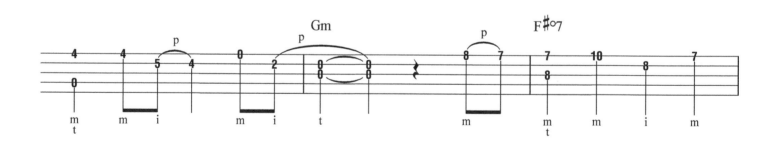

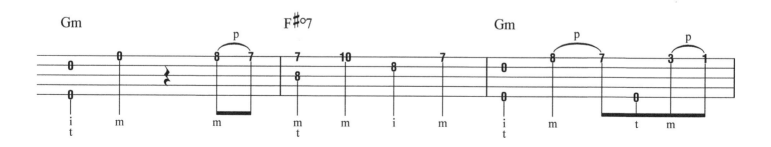

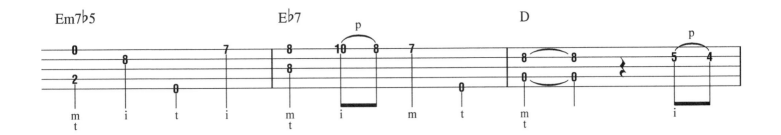

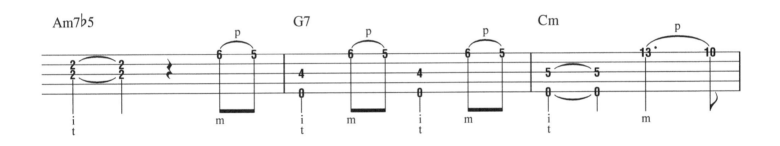

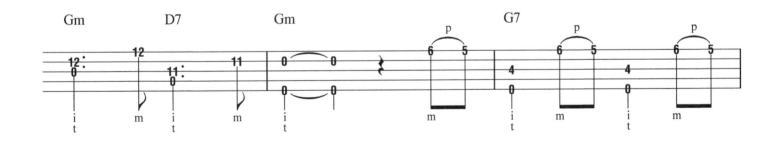

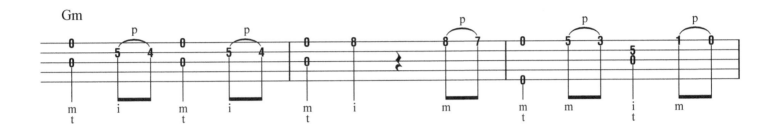

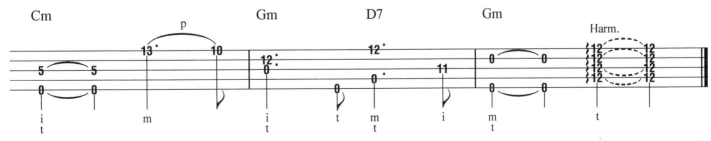

Trumpet Tune

By Henry Purcell

G tuning:
(5th-1st) G-D-G-B-D

Key of C

Moderately

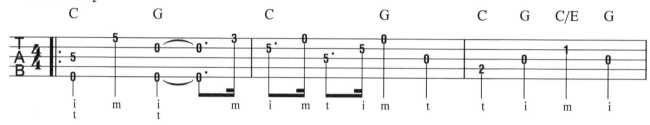

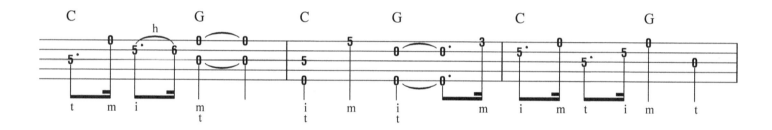

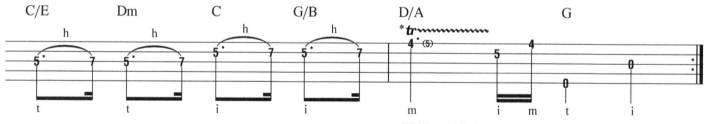

*Trill: Rapidly hammer on & pull off notes on 1st string.

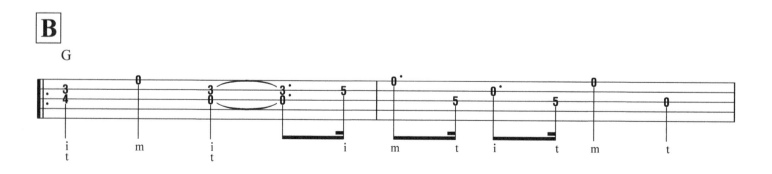

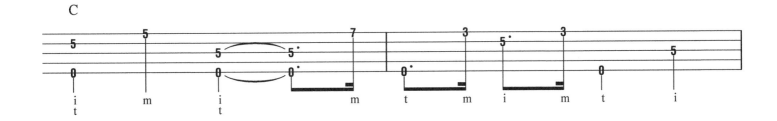

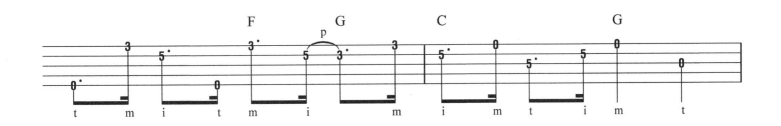

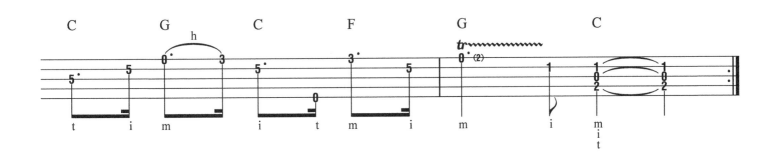

Trumpet Voluntary

By Jeremiah Clarke

G tuning:
(5th-1st) G-D-G-B-D

Key of C

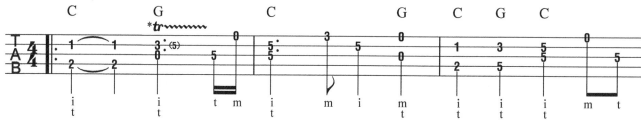

*Trill: Rapidly hammer on & pull off notes on 2nd string.

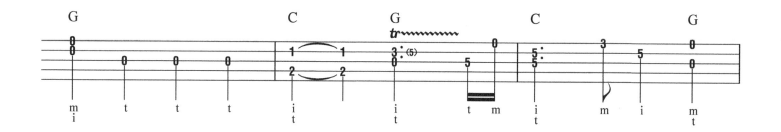

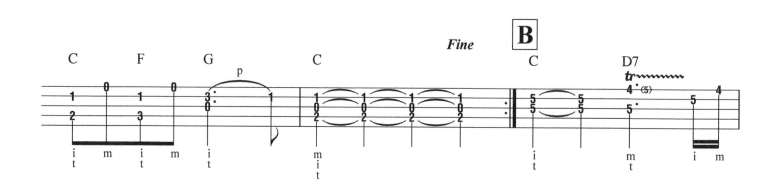

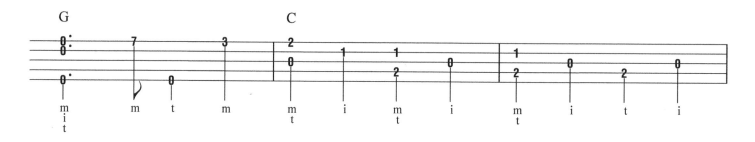

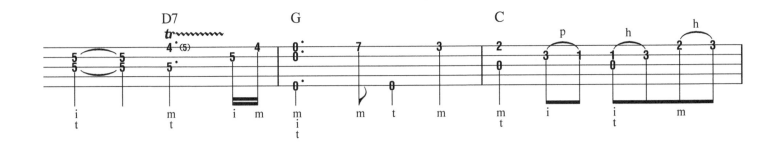

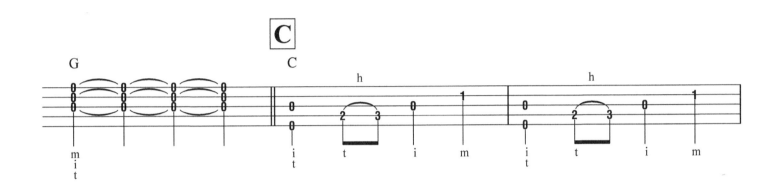

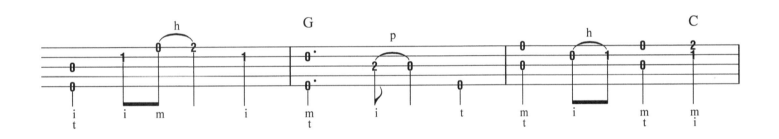

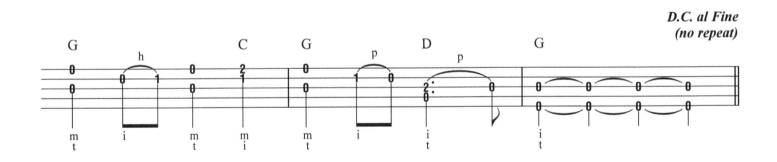

Theme from Swan Lake
(from *Swan Lake*)

By Pyotr Il'yich Tchaikovsky

G minor tuning:
(5th–1st) G-D-G-B♭-D

Key of G minor

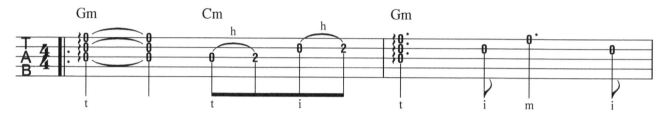

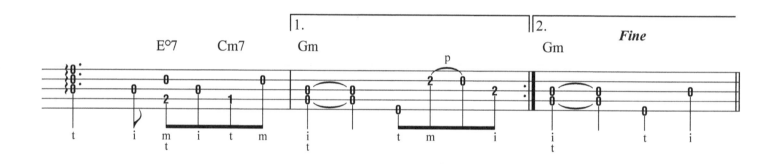

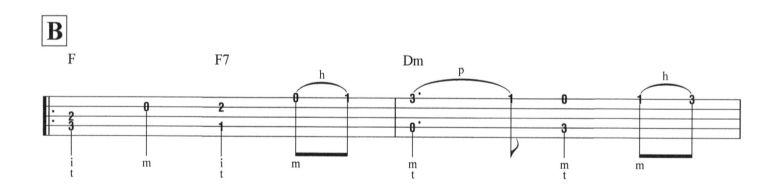

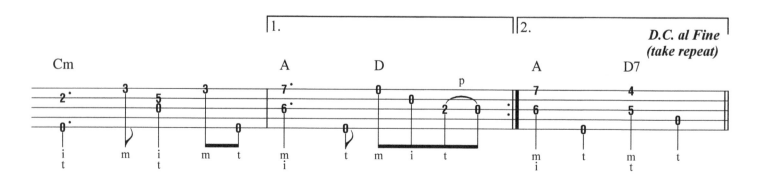

The Wild Horseman
(from *Album for the Young*)

By Robert Schumann

G tuning:
(5th-1st) G-D-G-B-D

Key of E minor

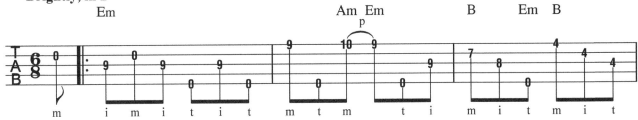

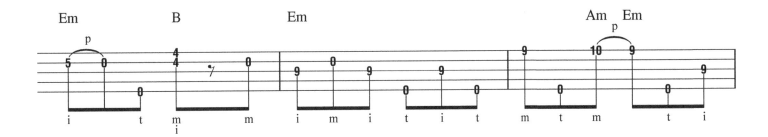

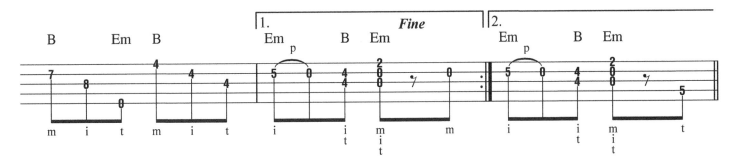

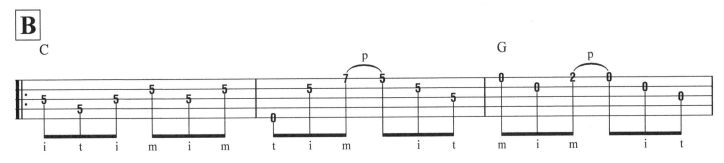

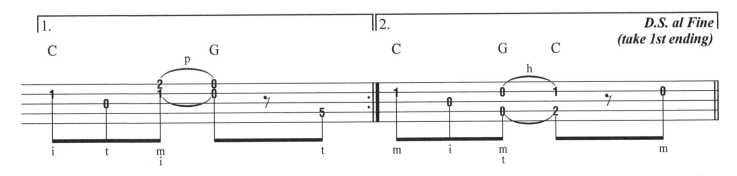

BANJO NOTATION LEGEND

TABLATURE graphically represents the banjo fingerboard. Each horizontal line represents a string, and each number represents a fret.

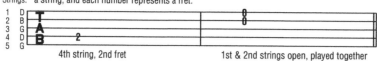

4th string, 2nd fret   1st & 2nd strings open, played together

TIME SIGNATURE:
The upper number indicates the number of beats per measure, the lower number indicates that a quarter note gets one beat.

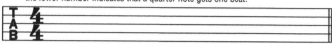

CUT TIME:
Each note's time value should be cut in half. As a result, the music will be played twice as fast as it is written.

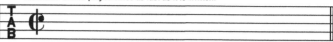

QUARTER NOTE:
time value = 1 beat

EIGHTH NOTES:
time value = 1/2 beat each

single   in series

SIXTEENTH NOTES:
time value = 1/4 beat each

single   in series

DOTTED QUARTER NOTE:
time value = 1 1/2 beat

TIE: Pick the 1st note only, then let it sustain for the combined time value.

TRIPLET: Three notes played in the same time normally occupied by two notes of the same time value.

GRACE NOTE: A quickly played note with no time value of its own. The grace note and the note following it only occupy the time value of the second note.

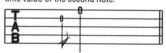

RITARD: A gradual slowing of the tempo or speed of the song.

QUARTER REST:
time value = 1 beat of silence

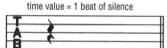

EIGHTH REST:
time value = 1/2 beat of silence

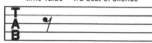

HALF REST:
time value = 2 beats of silence

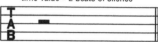

WHOLE REST:
time value = 4 beats of silence

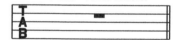

ENDINGS: When a repeated section has a first and second ending, play the first ending only the first time and play the second ending only the second time.

1.   2.

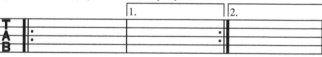
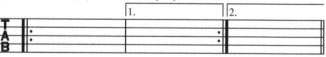

REPEAT SIGNS: Play the music between the repeat signs two times.

D.S. AL CODA:
Play through the music until you complete the measure labeled *"D.S. al Coda,"* then go back to the sign (𝄋).
Then play until you complete the measure labeled *"To Coda ⊕,"* then skip to the section labeled "⊕ Coda."

𝄋   *To Coda* ⊕   *D.S. al Coda*   ⊕ *Coda*

HAMMER-ON: Strike the first (lower) note with one finger, then sound the higher note (on the same string) with another finger by fretting it without picking.

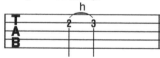

PULL-OFF: Place both fingers on the notes to be sounded. Strike the first note and without picking, pull the finger off to sound the second (lower) note.

SLIDE UP: Strike the first note and then slide the same fret-hand finger up to the second note. The second note is not struck.

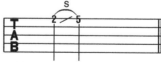

SLIDE DOWN: Strike the first note and then slide the same fret-hand finger down to the second note. The second note is not struck.

HALF-STEP CHOKE: Strike the note and bend the string up 1/2 step.

WHOLE-STEP CHOKE: Strike the note and bend the string up one step.

NATURAL HARMONIC: Strike the note while the fret-hand lightly touches the string directly over the fret indicated.

BRUSH: Play the notes of the chord indicated by quickly rolling them from bottom to top.

Scruggs/Keith Tuners:

HALF-TWIST UP: Strike the note, twist tuner up 1/2 step, and continue playing.

HALF-TWIST DOWN: Strike the note, twist tuner down 1/2 step, and continue playing.

WHOLE-TWIST UP: Strike the note, twist tuner up one step, and continue playing.

WHOLE-TWIST DOWN: Strike the note, twist tuner down one step, and continue playing.

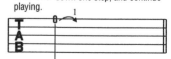

Right Hand Fingerings

t = thumb   i = index finger   m = middle finger

HAL•LEONARD® BANJO PLAY-ALONG

The Banjo Play-Along Series will help you play your favorite songs quickly and easily with incredible backing tracks to help you sound like a bona fide pro! Just follow the banjo tab, listen to the demo audio track provided to hear how the banjo should sound, and then play along with the separate backing tracks.

INCLUDES TAB

Each Banjo Play-Along pack features eight cream of the crop songs.

1. BLUEGRASS
Ashland Breakdown • Deputy Dalton • Dixie Breakdown • Hickory Hollow • I Wish You Knew • I Wonder Where You Are Tonight • Love and Wealth • Salt Creek.
00102585 Book/CD Pack $16.99

2. COUNTRY
East Bound and Down • Flowers on the Wall • Gentle on My Mind • Highway 40 Blues • If You've Got the Money (I've Got the Time) • Just Because • Take It Easy • You Are My Sunshine.
00105278 Book/CD Pack $14.99

3. FOLK/ROCK HITS
Ain't It Enough • The Cave • Forget the Flowers • Ho Hey • Little Lion Man • Live and Die • Switzerland • Wagon Wheel.
00119867 Book/CD Pack $14.99

4. OLD-TIME CHRISTMAS
Away in a Manger • Hark! the Herald Angels Sing • Jingle Bells • Joy to the World • O Holy Night • O Little Town of Bethlehem • Silent Night • We Wish You a Merry Christmas.
00119889 Book/CD Pack $14.99

5. PETE SEEGER
Blue Skies • Get up and Go • If I Had a Hammer (The Hammer Song) • Kisses Sweeter Than Wine • Mbube (Wimoweh) • Sailing Down My Golden River • Turn! Turn! Turn! (To Everything There Is a Season) • We Shall Overcome.
00129699 Book/CD Pack $17.99

6. SONGS FOR BEGINNERS
Bill Cheatham • Black Mountain Rag • Cripple Creek • Grandfather's Clock • John Hardy • Nine Pound Hammer • Old Joe Clark • Will the Circle Be Unbroken.
00139751 Book/CD Pack $14.99

7. BLUEGRASS GOSPEL
Cryin' Holy unto the Lord • How Great Thou Art • I Saw the Light • I'll Fly Away • I'll Have a New Life • Man in the Middle • Turn Your Radio On • Wicked Path of Sin.
00147594 Book/Online Audio $14.99

8. CELTIC BLUEGRASS
Billy in the Low Ground • Cluck Old Hen • Devil's Dream • Fisher's Hornpipe • Little Maggie • Over the Waterfall • The Red Haired Boy • Soldier's Joy.
00160077 Book/Online Audio $14.99

9. BLUEGRASS FESTIVAL FAVORITES
Banks of the Ohio • Cotton Eyed Joe • Cumberland Gap • Eighth of January • Liberty • Man of Constant Sorrow • Roll in My Sweet Baby's Arms • Wildwood Flower.
00263129 Book/Online Audio $14.99

HAL•LEONARD®
www.halleonard.com

Prices, contents, and availability subject to change without notice.

GREAT BANJO PUBLICATIONS

FROM HAL LEONARD

Hal Leonard Banjo Method – Second Edition

by Mac Robertson, Robbie Clement, Will Schmid
This innovative method teaches 5-string banjo bluegrass style using a carefully paced approach that keeps beginners playing great songs *while learning.* Book 1 covers easy chord strums, tablature, right-hand rolls, hammer-ons, slides and pull-offs, and more. Book 2 includes solos and licks, fiddle tunes, back-up, capo use, and more.
00699500 Book 1 Book Only $7.99
00695101 Book 1 Book/Online Audio $16.99
00699502 Book 2 Book Only $7.99

Banjo Aerobics
A 50-Week Workout Program for Developing, Improving and Maintaining Banjo Technique
by Michael Bremer
Take your banjo playing to the next level with this fantastic daily resource, providing a year's worth of practice material with a two-week vacation. The accompanying audio includes demo tracks for all the examples in the book to reinforce how the banjo should sound.
00113734 Book/Online Audio $19.99

Banjo Chord Finder
This extensive reference guide covers over 2,800 banjo chords, including four of the most commonly used tunings. Thirty different chord qualities are covered for each key, and each chord quality is presented in two different voicings. Also includes a lesson on chord construction and a fingerboard chart of the banjo neck!
00695741 9 x 12 .... $8.99   00695742 6 x 9 .... $6.99

Banjo Scale Finder
by Chad Johnson
Learn to play scales on the banjo with this comprehensive yet easy-to-use book. It contains more than 1,300 scale diagrams for the most often-used scales and modes, including multiple patterns for each scale. Also includes a lesson on scale construction and a fingerboard chart of the banjo neck.
00695780 9 x 12 .... $9.99   00695783 6 x 9 .... $6.99

First 50 Songs You Should Play on Banjo
arr. Michael J. Miles & Greg Cahill
Easy-to-read banjo tab, chord symbols and lyrics for the most popular songs banjo players like to play. Explore clawhammer and three-finger-style banjo in a variety of tunings and capoings with this one-of-a-kind collection. Songs include: Angel from Montgomery • Carolina in My Mind • Cripple Creek • Danny Boy • The House of the Rising Sun • Mr. Tambourine Man • Take Me Home, Country Roads • This Land Is Your Land • Wildwood Flower • and many more.
00153311 ....$14.99

Fretboard Roadmaps
by Fred Sokolow
This handy book/with online audio will get you playing all over the banjo fretboard in any key! You'll learn to: increase your chord, scale and lick vocabulary • play chord-based licks, moveable major and blues scales, melodic scales and first-position major scales • and much more! The audio includes 51 demonstrations of the exercises.
00695358 Book/Online Audio $15.99

O Brother, Where Art Thou?
Banjo tab arrangements of 12 bluegrass/folk songs from this Grammy-winning album. Includes: The Big Rock Candy Mountain • Down to the River to Pray • I Am a Man of Constant Sorrow • I Am Weary (Let Me Rest) • I'll Fly Away • In the Jailhouse Now • Keep on the Sunny Side • You Are My Sunshine • and more, plus lyrics and a banjo notation legend.
00699528 Banjo Tablature... $14.99

Earl Scruggs and the 5-String Banjo
Earl Scruggs' legendary method has helped thousands of banjo players get their start. It features everything you need to know to start playing, even how to build your own banjo! Topics covered include: Scruggs tuners • how to read music • chords • how to read tablature • anatomy of Scruggs-style picking • exercises in picking • 44 songs • biographical notes • and more! The online audio features Earl Scruggs playing and explaining over 60 examples!
00695764 Book Only.. $24.99
00695765 Book/Online Audio.. $34.99

Clawhammer Cookbook
Tools, Techniques & Recipes for Playing Clawhammer Banjo
by Michael Bremer
The goal of this book isn't to tell you how to play tunes or how to play like anyone else. It's to teach you ways to approach, arrange, and personalize any tune – to develop your own unique style. To that end, we'll take in a healthy serving of old-time music and also expand the clawhammer palate to taste a few other musical styles. Includes audio track demos of all the songs and examples to aid in the learning process.
00118354 Book/Online Audio...$19.99

The Ultimate Banjo Songbook
A great collection of banjo classics: Alabama Jubilee • Bye Bye Love • Duelin' Banjos • The Entertainer • Foggy Mountain Breakdown • Great Balls of Fire • Lady of Spain • Orange Blossom Special • (Ghost) Riders in the Sky • Rocky Top • San Antonio Rose • Tennessee Waltz • UFO-TOFU • You Are My Sunshine • and more.
00699565 Book/Online Audio.. $27.50

HAL•LEONARD®